the **Duct Tape Guys**

present

THE ORIGINAL
DUCT TAPE
HALLOWEEN

SO CREATIVE
IT'S SCARY!

BOOK

by Jim and Tim, the Duct Tape Guys

Workman Publishing • New York

Text: Tim Nyberg and Jim Berg
Design, models, and illustrations: Tim Nyberg
Photography: Scott Olson, Tim Nyberg

Library of Congress Cataloging-in-Publication Data
is available.
ISBN 0-7611-3187-6

Workman books are available at special discounts when
purchased in bulk for premiums and sales promotions
as well as for fund-raising or educational use. Special
editions or book excerpts can also be created to
specification. For details, contact the Special Sales
Director at the address below.

Workman Publishing Company, Inc.
708 Broadway
New York, NY 10003-9555
www.workman.com

Manufactured in the United States of America

First printing: August 2003

10 9 8 7 6 5 4 3 2 1

Acknowledgments

Thanks to Workman Publishing for once again lowering their standards and allowing two dumb guys to evangelize the "Gospel of Duct Tape." Thanks to our families and friends, who are always supportive of (or at least acting mildly interested in) our efforts. Thanks to the Department of Homeland Security for their wonderful job of bringing duct tape to the forefront of American consciousness in February of 2003. Thanks to the myriad duct tape enthusiasts around the world who have been so supportive and taken time to share their duct tape stories on our web site: www.ducttapeguys.com. And finally, thanks to Henkel Consumer Adhesives, who have provided us with all of the Duck® brand duct tape that has been used in the creation of the costumes and props shown in this book.

– *Jim and Tim, the Duct Tape Guys*

"Hey, Tim. Aren't we supposed to thank the Academy or something?"

"Not yet, Jim. Wait until our movie comes out."

"Hey, Tim. Why is this page blank?"

"It's supposed to be. At least that's what it says in the Chicago Manual of Style."

"Seems like a waste of paper to me, Tim."

"Thanks to your question, Jim, that's no longer an issue."

We Love Halloween

Jim and I have always loved Halloween—mainly because it's the only time of year when people don't stare at us and think we're dressed strangely. Having raised five kids between the two of us, we have a lot of trick-or-treating under our belts, and a heck of a lot of Halloween candy, too... which may help explain our expanding girth. At any rate, we thought that we'd depart from our typical duct tape hints for this, our sixth book, and share our favorite duct tape Halloween ideas.

Enjoy!

over
101
clever
COSTUME IDEAS

Notice that we say "clever" costume ideas, as in creative. Let this then be your warning that all of these costumes may not be practical. In fact, some of them might be downright painful (even dangerous). So, grab on to the usable ideas and consider the rest of them as just plain stupid ideas meant to amuse you and fill 128 pages.

Disclaimer

Like our other books, *The Original Duct Tape Halloween Book* contains humor. Please don't try any of the stuff in this book that seems blatantly stupid, potentially injurious, disrespectful to human or animal life, or outright dangerous. Some of our ideas are real, usable ideas (you figure out which ones). You may want to try some of these ideas or you may not. Whatever the case, you're hereby notified that you're doing so at your own risk. Other ideas in this book have been deemed "breathtakingly stupid" and therefore are obviously for entertainment purposes only (assuming you find extremely stupid stuff entertaining).

All brand names mentioned in this book are the registered trademarks of their respective owners. Just because they are mentioned in this book doesn't mean that these companies are endorsing what we are suggesting.

Finally, when applying duct tape to your skin, be ready to have some pain and hair loss upon its removal. And, if you get duct tape tangled up in your hair, you may be in for the scariest experience of your entire life.

- Jim and Tim, the Duct Tape Guys

P.S. We will not be held responsible for sudden cardiovascular trauma that may be experienced when viewing some of the really scary photos in this book—like Tim in the pink hooded sweat suit on page 4.

Basic Training:
Duct Tape Cloth

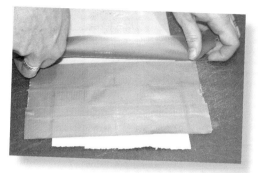

Most of these costumes require "duct tape cloth." This is easy to make if you have a Formica countertop. All you have to do is lay down strips of duct tape overlapping each other by about 1/4 inch. Carefully peel the duct tape sheet off the counter, flip it over, and tape the other side in the same overlapping manner. For extra-strong cloth, tape the back side at a 90-degree angle to the tape on the first side.

You can save duct tape by taping over one side of lightweight (for flexibility) plastic sheeting or a garbage bag.

When you've created your duct tape cloth, you can trim it to the size and shape you need—just like you do when cutting a clothing pattern out of cloth.

The Scare Tactics listed throughout this book present ideas for using duct tape to create your own decorations, special effects, and other ways to "haunt" the house for Halloween.

If you're like us, and we know we are, you're always looking for a shortcut (mostly so you can get back to the couch more quickly). These construction tips all have been thoroughly tested by us for speed and efficiency.

Basic Training:
Cutting Duct Tape

It is generally easiest to rip duct tape with your hands, rather than cutting it with a scissors or knife. If you need a clean edge to your cut, we recommend using an X-Acto knife on a cutting board.

Basic Training:
Head Wrapping

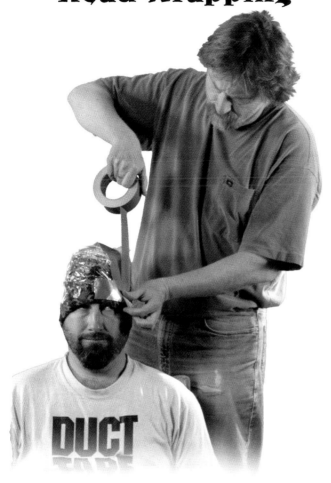

To prevent pain and hair loss when making a duct tape mask, hat, cowl, or turban, wrap your head in paper toweling and/or plastic wrap prior to applying the duct tape. For turbans, pad out the shape with crumpled newspapers prior to taping.

3

GENERAL STUPIDITY
from the Duct Tape Guys

Save money on Halloween treats this year. Rip duct tape into short strips, give them a twist, and pass them out to the kids, telling them it's "Space Jerky"!

Scattered throughout this book you will see the 30-Second Costume icon. This is your cue to a quick and easy costume idea—perfect for those of you who are procrastinators, or just plain forgetful and need to leave for a party in a few minutes.

30-second costume:
Used Bubble Gum

Dress entirely in pink or minty green, duct tape a shoe to your head, and go trick-or-treating as used bubble gum.

Air Freshener

Cut a giant pine tree out of cardboard and cover it with green duct tape. Put a string in the top of the tree and hang it around your neck.

Vegas Best Man

Create a colorfully gaudy duct tape tux and you're ready to be the best man at a Vegas wedding, host a game show, or pull a rabbit out of a hat.

Dirty Dozen

Fill an egg carton with dirtied hard-boiled or plastic eggs and duct tape the carton to your head.

"That's stupid, Jim."

"Then don't do it, Tim. Duh!"

Giant Spider
Cover two Styrofoam balls (or wadded-up newspaper) with black duct tape to form the body of the spider. Attach eight legs made out of rolled black or silver duct tape. Two small, red duct tape balls make scary eyes. Attach to web on page 5.

The Human Shower

Suspend a hula hoop over your head by duct taping it to a broomstick that's duct taped securely to your back. Tape a showerhead to the broomstick, and attach a shower curtain to the hula hoop. Walk around singing your favorite songs.

Kissing Booth

Attach a sprig of mistletoe to an L-shaped bracket and duct tape the whole thing to your forehead. Presto! You're a portable kissing booth. Add an optional sign, "Kisses $1."

Can't find any mistletoe? Do like Tim does—make your own using green and white duct tape.

A Noisy Joke

Sneak up to someone's house in the middle of the night and duct tape their doorbell down (assuming they have a bell that keeps making noise as long as the button is depressed). When they go to the front door to figure out what's wrong with the bell, sneak around to the back of the house and do the same. Repeat.

Bouncer at a Speakeasy

Take the lid of a shoe box (or similar size cardboard), cut a one-inch by six-inch slit in the middle of it, and tape it to your head so your eyes look out of the slit. You are now the bouncer at a speakeasy! "What's the password?"

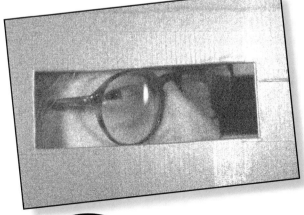

Baked Potato

Cover a puffy down ski jacket with silver duct tape, with brown duct tape around your shoulders and neck area, and go trick-or-treating as a baked potato!

Note: Don't forget the pat of butter and dollop of sour cream on your head—created, of course, with yellow and white duct tape.

11

Are you of a size that you don't need a puffy ski jacket? Are you concerned about calories? Wrap your candy entirely in duct tape before you eat it. This will effectively seal in the calories and fat content.

Siamese Twins

Duct tape yourself to your best friend or spouse (both, as the case may be) and go to the Halloween party as Siamese twins.

Note: Jim and Tim both recommend against doing this with your brother-in-law.

Floor of a Movie Theater

Make yourself a sticky-side-out duct tape vest. Cover the vest with popcorn kernels, candy wrappers, straws, and crushed paper cups. Don't forget the Jujubes!

Don't leave your family pet out of the trick-or-treating fun! Turn your dog into a Siamese dog by duct taping a stuffed dog onto its back. The perfect companion(s) for the Siamese Twin costume on page 12!

30-second costume:
Missing Person

Cut a circle out of one side of a paper milk carton and write the words "Have You Seen Me?" under the hole. Cut out the bottom of the carton and make a slit up the side opposite the circle. Duct tape this contraption around your head with your face peering out of the circular hole.

Skeleton

Skulls and Skeletons
Crumpled newspaper, cardboard tubing, and white and black duct tape are the only things you need to create skulls and skeletons for your haunted house.

Black pants and a black turtleneck with white duct tape "bones" make a quick and easy skeleton costume. Or, use silver duct tape to make a "Terminator" skeleton.

15

Chia Pet

Cover yourself in duct tape (sticky side out) and roll around on freshly mowed grass: Presto! You're a Chia Pet!
If freshly mowed grass isn't available, you can use green Easter basket grass.

Wolfman

Be safe and light the way. When you're trick-or-treating, duct tape a flashlight to your arm, leg, or head to light your path and warn cars.

"That ain't stupid, Tim!"

"I didn't say it was, Jim."

Your sticky-side-out duct tape vest quickly turns into a cool wolfman or werewolf outfit when you roll around on the barbershop floor. Add a black duct tape nose to your face and you are ready to go howl at the moon!

17

Hot Dog Vendor

Fashion a neck strap out of duct tape and attach it to a silver duct tape–covered Styrofoam cooler so you can sling it around your neck. Write "Hot Dogs" on the front of the cooler. Make a duct tape hinge for the back side of the cooler lid. For the look of a real hot dog vendor, make a white duct tape vendor's cap. Your trick-or-treat treats can be collected in the cooler.

Additional Hot Dog Vendor hint:
Cut a hole through the back of the cooler big enough for you to stick your arm through. Inside, you'll be operating a dog hand puppet. When you ring the doorbell, have the dog puppet pop out of the box and say, "Trick or treat! Man, is it HOT in here!"

Disco Lives!

Duct tape little mirrors all over yourself and you'll be the ball of the ball. And good news: The rounder you are, the more authentic this costume will be.

HALLOWEEN party Hint

Insert small candies into several balloons, then blow them up. Duct tape the balloons together into whatever shape you choose. Use duct tape to hang the candy-filled beast from the ceiling. Blindfold contestants and have them flail around with a stick until the balloon beast spills its contents, one body cavity at a time.

Aphenphosmphobe*

Duct tape a hula hoop to your shoulders to ensure that your personal space is not violated.

"Aphenphosmphobe*?! That's a twenty-dollar word, Tim!"

"Actually, I got it on sale. It was only $17.98!"

*Someone with a fear of being touched.

Duct Tape Biker

Giant Bat
Black duct tape wings on a duct tape-covered crumpled newspaper body. A coathanger wire keeps the wings up. Hang with black thread. *The one shown below has a four-foot wingspan!*

Cover your pants and jacket in black duct tape and make a white duct tape skull and crossbones on your back. Duct tape a set of handlebars onto your belt (and optionally, add your "ol' lady" to your back).

21

Warning: For each of these costumes it is advised that you wear a body stocking or cover yourself in tan duct tape first if you don't want to spend the night in jail.

Adam and/or Eve

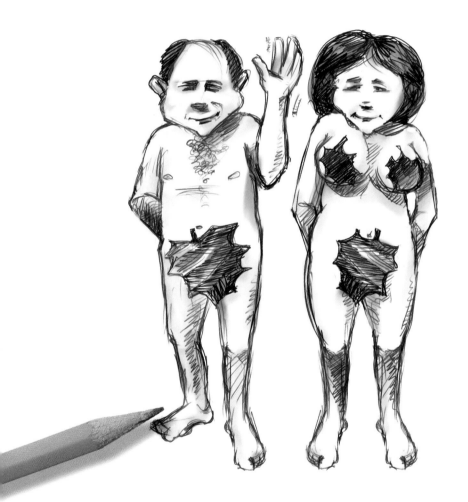

Make a big duct tape leaf and secure it over your privates. For Eve, make three duct tape leaves.

Invisible Man

SCARE TACTICS

Invisible Dog

Duct tape a straightened-out wire coat hanger to a dog collar. Wrap the wire in duct tape to make it look like a leash. Presto! Invisible dog!

Cover yourself in camouflage duct tape and go to the party as the invisible man.

Note: This only works if the party is being held in a jungle or heavily wooded area. If you're indoors, try to find out the color of the party room, then wrap yourself in a matching color of duct tape.

23

30-second costume:
Politician

Duct tape a photo of an extra mouth to the other side of your face.

"I don't get it, Tim!"

"Politicians are said to talk out of both sides of their face."

"So?"

"Go away, Jim."

Note: For extra realism, stuff your pockets with special-interest money.

Doggie Doo Head

Vacant House

Create that "nobody's home" look by duct taping black paper over your windows. No black paper? Use black duct tape—your windows will be totally dirt free (possibly even glass free) when you remove it.

The original lawn ornament. Create a brown duct tape turban to which you attach giant duct tape flies.

Editor's Note: The publisher wishes to apologize for this costume idea. Unfortunately, we didn't notice it until the book was already printed.

Vegas-Era Elvis

Black duct tape makes a great Elvis 'do, complete with muttonchop sideburns and ducktail flip in the back. To achieve the correct Elvis stance, duct tape your knees together. To create your Vegas-era Elvis outfit, find a paisley tux like Jim's, or make a basic white duct tape tux. Add silver duct tape to the lapels.

Notes: To achieve the Elvis sunglasses we just enhanced the rims of Jim's sunglasses with yellow duct tape. Those who can't do the Elvis sneer can use duct tape to keep their upper lip in the proper position.

Marilyn Monroe

Even More Noise

This one will set you back the price of an air horn, but will cause a lot of commotion! Duct tape down the trigger on an air horn and toss it onto a roof!

A tight wrapping of white duct tape over your upper torso and a permanently flying-away dress on your lower half turns you into Marilyn over the subway grate—just build some stiff wire into the hem of the skirt. If you don't have Monroe's blonde hair, you can create the bombshell look with yellow duct tape.

27

Nasty Razor Face

To simulate a horrible shaving accident, apply a short strip of red duct tape to your face and attach a disposable razor to the bottom edge of the tape.

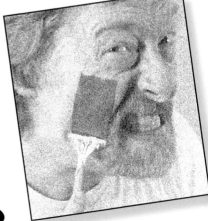

28

Human Duct Tape Dispenser
(or, Repair Anything Guy)

 **Fun Fact:** Jim wears this contraption every day of his life.

Use PVC pipes and/or wood to create a dispenser that holds three or four rolls of duct tape. You are now ready to repair anything.

Scary Windows
Make "cracked windows" by cutting white duct tape into little strips and applying to windows in a crack pattern.

Pro Wrestler

Make a duct tape hooded mask. Strip down to your massive, potbellied Duct Tape Guy glory and try to flex a lot.

Note: An easy way to make a duct tape hood is to duct tape over a midsize grocery bag.

Baby Back Ribs

Duct tape several baby dolls together and fasten them to your back, along your spine. (Barbecue sauce is optional.)

30-second costume:
Face-Lift

You can easily achieve the look of an aging Hollywood movie star by pulling back your facial skin with duct tape, simulating costly plastic surgery.

Warning: You are virtually guaranteed some pain and hair loss during removal.

Gals: You can achieve cleavage of Oscar Night proportions using strategically placed duct tape.

Giraffe

Note:
Remember to duck as you go through doors.

Create a cardboard giraffe neck and head covered with yellow duct tape for the basic color and brown duct tape for the spots. Cut a hole in the front of the neck so you can see. Cover a yellow turtleneck with matching brown giraffe-pattern spots. Green duct tape foliage hanging from the giraffe's mouth adds to the effect.

SCARE TACTICS

Tombstone Yard Decorations

Cardboard cut into tombstone shapes and covered with silver duct tape makes for an authentic looking (and weatherproof) tombstone. Add names with a marker or black duct tape.

33

Wrap your candy-grabbing hand in duct tape, sticky side out, so when you help yourself from the candy bowls, you'll be grabbing up to three times as much candy.

Alien

Cover yourself in green duct tape. Add scales, tail, extra limbs as desired. Or, use classic silver duct tape like Bruce Larsen of Fairhope, Alabama, did with his duct tape alien.

My Favorite Martian

Duct tape television antennae to the back of your head and, presto! You are a vintage 1960s Martian (à la Ray Walston).

Hint: For static-free reception from the red planet, duct tape a static-free dryer sheet to your antenna.

Haz-Mat Suit

Cover yourself from neck to toe with bright yellow duct tape. Cover a paper grocery bag with the tape, cut a square hole in the front, and use a contrasting color of tape, if you like, to secure a plastic "window" in place (a sheet of transparency material works well for this). Place bag over your head and you are prepared to deal with any chemical or biohazard cleanup.

"Duct Tape: Homeland Security on a Roll!"

Kangaroo

Affix a big brown duct tape tail (crumpled newspaper covered in brown duct tape) to your behind, then duct tape a grocery bag to your belly in which to collect treats. Hop from door to door.

Answer the Phone!

Halloween party prank: Wedge a little duct tape around the "talk" button on the handset cradle of your party host's phone. This ensures that the phone will keep ringing even after it's picked up.

Headless Guy

Wadded newspaper pads out shoulders and arms.

Duct tape two boxes to your shoulders, tall enough so they're even with the top of your head. Pull a turtleneck over them, then a sport coat. If the turtleneck is thin enough, you should be able to see through without cutting any holes in it.

Human Newsstand

Make a duct tape vest and cover it with magazines and newspapers. For additional effect, secure a cardboard box at belt level and stick a few magazines around the edges. This also makes a good candy collection device.

Postal Carrier

Note: For added realism, act disgruntled.

Dress in a blue suit, or cover an old suit with blue duct tape. Duct tape a stuffed dog to your leg, mouth first. Make a big mail sack out of tan or brown duct tape. Arrange a few letters around the opening of the sack. This sack is great for collecting your Halloween treats.

Dust Bunny

SCARE TACTICS

Man-Eating Plant

Use colored duct tape to create a large man-eating plant, à la Audrey 2 in *Little Shop of Horrors*. Tape over rolled-up newspapers to form the stems.

A plastic hand coming out of the plant's "mouth" adds to the horror.

Wrap your body in duct tape, sticky side out, and roll around under the beds in your house. This accomplishes your annual cleaning and creates a great "dust bunny" costume. Finish it off with a couple of duct tape rabbit ears.

Silly Putty

Note: For extra, extra realism, duct tape a page from your newspaper's color comic section to your back.

Wrap yourself entirely in beige (light tan) duct tape and go as Silly Putty. For extra realism, duct tape halves of a plastic egg to your head and butt.

Refrigerator Magnet

Create a lightweight refrigerator by covering a refrigerator-sized box with white duct tape. Make handles out of cardboard covered in silver and black duct tape. Duct tape this whole assembly to your back and go as a refrigerator magnet.

43

Thirty-Point Buck

Miniature Ghost Attack!

Tie a cotton ball to a strong black thread about six feet long. Attach the other end of the thread to a piece of duct tape, sticky side up. Lay the duct tape on the sidewalk leading up to a house. When a trick-or-treater steps on the tape, it will stick to their shoe and they'll have a small white ghost following them around.

Duct tape branches to your head and go as a buck. Add a red duct tape nose and you're Rudolph the Red-Nosed Reindeer.

Human Pencil Sharpener

Using yellow, red, and silver duct tape, make a giant pencil out of cardboard tubing. Duct tape this pencil to your chest, eraser end out. You are a human pencil sharpener.

45

Hilarious DUCT TAPE PRANK

Bathroom Water Issues

Go to one of those public bathrooms that have sensor toilets and put a small piece of duct tape over the sensor so the toilet never flushes, or put it over the sensor on the sink so the water is always on. Black duct tape does the trick nicely—it blends right in with the lens.

GENERAL STUPIDITY

from the Duct Tape Guys

"You could go trick-or-treating as Father Thyme. . . . just make a sticky-side-out duct tape vest and cover yourself in thyme."

"I'm pretty sure it's Father Time, Jim. You know, time like on a clock?"

"Oh. Well, how about Father Oregano then?"

"Don't you have somewhere you're supposed to be, Jim?"

Lincoln Log

Wrap yourself from neck to toe in brown duct tape and make yourself a black Abraham Lincoln beard and a stovepipe hat.

Note: For added authenticity, put a beige duct tape mole on your right cheek.

Used Dental Floss

Dress in white and duct tape random bits of food to your body. Run some folded white duct tape in one ear and out the other and you have "Mental Floss!"

Metallic Mummy

Cover yourself head to toe in duct tape and speak in inaudible groans—which won't be too hard when you're totally encased in duct tape. Feeling old-fashioned? Go with traditional mummy-white duct tape.

Warning: We recommend duct taping over long johns or tight-fitting clothing or you'll be in a world of pain—and totally hairless—when you remove the costume.

Rainbow

Note: Bend over with your potted head touching the ground to form a rainbow.

Fill a plastic pot with yellow duct tape nuggets and wear it inverted on your head. Cover the rest of your body in a rainbow of different-colored duct tape stripes.

"Hey, he looks like a pothead, Tim!"

"Very funny, Jim."

Speaking of rainbows . . . Here are four costumes based on one of our favorite movies of all time: *The Wizard of Oz.*

Tin Man Follow the instructions for the mummy costume (page 48), but don't tape over your face. Instead, duct tape a funnel to the top of your head and carry around an oil can and ax.

The WIZARD of OZ Character

Scarecrow Duct tape straw (or yellow duct tape strips) to your wrists and ankles. Make colored duct tape "patches" on your face.

Cowardly Lion

Fashion a brown or yellow duct tape mane to wear on your head, a black duct tape nose, and a long brown duct tape tail—which you hold on to for comfort.

The WIZARD of OZ Character

Yellow Brick Road Cover
yourself with yellow duct tape arranged in brick shapes, allowing your clothes to show through as the mortar lines.

Wind Chimes

If you live in Chicago, this is the perfect costume to take advantage of the wind in your windy city. If you live where there is no wind, consider bringing a fan and a really long extension cord trick-or-treating with you.

Duct tape various sizes of metal or plastic tubing to your arms and trick-or-treat as a wind chime.

Mermaid/Merman

Cover your legs with duct tape "scales" and make a big duct tape fin, half of which covers each foot.

Note: Weather and local ordinances permitting, you could go topless or duct tape scales to your T-shirt or tube top.

Edward Scissorhands

Duct tape scissors to your hands.

Warning: For safety, kids, always use blunt-end scissors. And remember, NO RUNNING with scissors! Therefore plan for extra time when trick-or-treating with this costume.

Howard Officesupplyhands*

Duct tape a stapler, paper punch, ruler, and other office supplies to your hands.

*Edward Scissorhands's half brother.

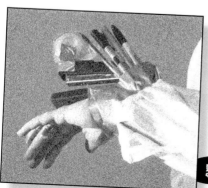

57

California Prunes

The California Raisins are a thing of the past. With our growing senior population, the California Prunes are going to be all the rage. Grab some brown and black duct tape and some crumpled newspaper and wrap yourself into a prune body. Don a gray wig and granny glasses or an old-man hat and you're stylin' as the fruit of choice for the geriatric generation.

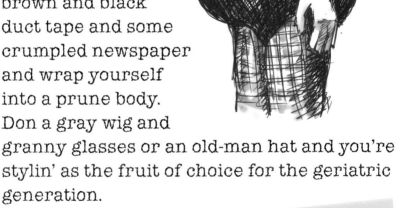

Note: Remember, nothing says "Old Guy" better than wearing mixed plaids. Make your own plaid apparel with duct tape!

Island Hoppers

An ordinary plastic tumbler turns into a fancy tropical tumbler when you wrap it with newspaper covered with brown duct tape—it will look kind of like a coconut. Add a little duct tape umbrella and a straw and you're good to go.

Long strips of green duct tape folded over onto itself makes a great Hawaiian skirt. Brown duct tape over your bra can replicate the look of a coconut shell bikini top. Have your guy make a Hawaiian shirt with colorful duct tape patterns on an ordinary short-sleeve shirt and you two are ready to hula!

59

Human ATM

Creepy Lamps

Use duct tape to create spider and bat silhouettes on the inside of lampshades.

Get a box large enough to cover your head and wrap it in silver duct tape. Cut out a hole large enough to reveal your face and hang a twenty-dollar bill out of your mouth. Presto! You've become the human ATM! (Dads of teenagers will relate to this.)

Luge Guy

Duct tape

yourself tightly from head to toe. Make little sled runners out of cardboard covered in silver duct tape and attach them to your back. You are now the human luge.

Warning: Again, duct taping over long johns is recommended, rather than over bare skin.

GENERAL STUPIDITY
from the Duct Tape Guys

You might have noticed that this and the next two costume ideas have "guy" in their title. This doesn't mean that they won't work on "gals" too. It just means that we're more apt to call either sex "guys."

Yeah, you know, like, "Hey guys, how's it going?"

Thanks for letting us clear that up.

Refrigerator Poetry Guy

Cover yourself with little strips of white duct tape with words written on them. All night long, your friends can have fun arranging sentences and poetry on your body.

30-second costume:
Strained Voice Guy

Duct tape a vegetable strainer in front of your mouth and you'll be "straining your voice" all night long without even shouting.

"That's really stupid, Tim."

"Thanks, Jim."

Two-Headed Hunchback

Duct tape a small child or little person to your back and go as a "hunchbacked, two-headed guy."

Note: If you can't locate a child or little person, decapitate a department store mannequin and duct tape its head to one of your shoulders.

Batman

Blue and black duct tape create the perfect form-fitting Batman cowl. A black cape with blue lining finishes the outfit.

Knight in Shining Armor

Cover yourself head to toe in silver duct tape (like the Metallic Mummy, page 48). Then add knee and elbow coverings made with cardboard wrapped in more silver duct tape. For your helmet, use the cowl construction method and add a face mask (more cardboard covered with silver duct tape). Remember your lance!

Dragon

The knight will need a dragon to slay. Make the head out of cardboard duct taped to the bill of a baseball cap. Cover the whole thing with green duct tape scales (see diagram). Big Styrofoam balls covered with white and black duct tape make the eyes, and red duct tape makes the tongue. Cover the rest of your suit with more green scales. Don't forget the tail.

Note: This can also be the foundation for a neat dinosaur costume.

News Anchor

Create a duct tape hairpiece in the traditional lacquered news anchor style. Duct tape a box to look like a television set and wear it over your head. Pepper your dialogue with lines like, "Our top story tonight ..." and "We'll be right back."

Evangelist

We've always considered ourselves "Duct Tape Evangelists," spreading the "gospel of duct tape." Some visitors at our web site have suggested that there be a duct tape religion. While we definitely believe duct tape is a gift from God, actually worshipping the silver roll goes a bit too far.

Duct tape several pocket testaments together to make a "Bible belt." It makes a great witnessing tool, too: Just rip off the testaments and pass them out. For authenticity, you may want to consider adding the "news anchor hairpiece" described previously.

Nun

Dress entirely in black and make a collar and wimple using white and black duct tape. Not Catholic and need visual? Rent *The Sound of Music.*

Nun Chucks

30-second costume:
Priest

Wear all black, including a black turtleneck. Fold a little strip of white duct tape over the front of your collar. Instant priest!

GENERAL STUPIDITY
from the Duct Tape Guys

Here's a Ninja Priest idea: Accessorize this outfit by duct taping two small nuns together. Swing 'em around and threaten people with your "nun chucks." (Pictured on page 70.)

Note: Can't find any small nuns? Get a couple of dolls and make habits and wimples for them out of black and white duct tape.

Ninja Farmer

Wear denim or bib overalls and carry a homemade martial arts device made from two rubber chickens duct taped together beak to beak. Swing 'em around and refer to your "numb clucks" as deadly weapons!

"Hey, Tim, you look just like Cluck Norris!"

"It's like poultry in motion, Jim!"

30-second costume:
Advertising Executive

Cover yourself in magazine ads.
When someone asks what you are, answer,
"I'm in advertising."

Ghoulish Surgeon

Duct tape a mirror to a headband and don your hospital scrubs. Fasten a few rolls of duct tape and a hacksaw to your belt and carry around a meat cleaver and a bunch of plastic severed limbs, with red duct tape over their stumps to simulate blood.

Human Flotation Device

Attach empty plastic pop bottles and milk jugs with duct tape around your upper torso and go trick-or-treating as a human flotation device.

Booby Trap Rigging

Use duct tape to rig those "booby trap" firecrackers (shown below) to the bottom of the screen door of the house that you just trick-or-treated at. Hide in the bushes and wait for the door to open. . . . BANG!

Campfire

Note: Walk around holding a hot dog or marshmallow on a stick over your head.

Cover an old sport coat with bright red, orange, and yellow duct tape flames. Make a flame-shaped cap for your head and duct tape your pant legs to look like logs.

Body Builder

Duct tape a six-pack of beer or pop to your belly and you're instantly sporting "six-pack abs."

"Hey, Jim. Looks more like you're sportin' a whole case!"

"Shut up, Tim!"

Etch-A-Sketch

Get two big sheets of cardboard. Cover one with red duct tape (this is the back) and the other with silver with a red border (this is the front). Use two empty duct tape rolls covered with white duct tape to make the knobs. Hang the sheets over your shoulders with duct tape straps, like a sandwich board.

Dirty Old Man

Wear a gray wig, an old-man driving cap, and mixed plaid clothing. Top it off with a duct tape vest, sticky side out, covered with dirt.

79

Hippie

Create a duct tape vest with fringes (make
sure you have a peace sign on the back),
duct tape–enhanced bell-bottom pants, and
a duct tape headband (braiding colored
duct tape strips adds to the authenticity).
Accessorize with a beaded necklace made
with little colored duct tape balls.

30-second costume:
Van Gogh

Have someone cover your back with duct tape and then quickly rip it off. When you are letting out your scream of pain, quickly duct tape your face into its contorted position. You'll look like that guy in the Munch painting, *The Scream.*

Become that famous Dutch painter in an instant by carrying a paintbrush and palette and putting a piece of duct tape over one ear.

Don't have a palette? Cut a cardboard shape and apply colored duct tape.

81

Seven Dwarfs

Cut out the backs of shoes and duct tape the fronts onto your knees and the knees of six of your friends. Make cone-shaped hats and beards out of duct tape.

Fifties Chick

Make your own poodle skirt, a wide A-line skirt adorned with duct tape poodle designs. Make saddle shoes with white and black duct tape. And don't forget your hula hoop!

SCARE TACTICS

Rundown House

If you want to create really realistic dilapidated siding on your house, duct tape over your siding and then rip off the tape—which will, in turn, remove paint, and much of the siding with it.

Duct tape corncobs all over your body. When people ask what you are, reply, "I'm all ears."

"That's WAY too stupid to put in the book, Jim!"

"Sorry, Tim."

Toothpaste

Make a large sheet of white duct tape and write "toothpaste" on it using red duct tape. Wrap it around your body and connect it to your neck using silver duct tape. Make a fez-like cap out of white duct tape for your head.

Hockey Player

Cover your front teeth with black duct tape. For added realism, make a "pocket mullet" by duct taping a wig into a duct tape headband (like Jim is wearing here). Also, create your own custom jersey with any duct tape color combination.

C.E.O. Duct Tape
Hair Club for Men

Warning: Do not apply directly to your head unless you are completely bald, or you will lose what little hair you have left. See page 3 for more instructions.

Make yourself some duct tape hair and go to the party as the founder of the Duct Tape Hair Club for Men. Get your pitch ready. "Duct Tape Hair: You can swim in it, ski in it, even bowl in it with complete confidence. The Duct Tape Hair Club for Men—Your loss is their gain."

30-second costume:
King of Remotes
(It's a guy thing.)

Duct tape several television and VCR remote controls to your arms. Nothing says "I'm the Man of the House" like control of the remotes.

SCARE TACTICS

Coffin

Cut cardboard into coffin shapes (shown below) and assemble with black duct tape. Hinge and add handles with silver duct tape, and line the coffin with red or white duct tape. You'll never find a cheaper coffin.

Pirate

Make a duct tape hook and tape it over one hand. Make a peg leg by covering a mailing tube in brown duct tape and taping it to your knee. A red pirate suit and black hat with a skull and crossbones will finish off the ensemble. Oh, and don't forget the black duct tape eye patch.

The Big Cheese

You don't have to be from Wisconsin to enjoy being a big wedge of cheese. Grab three hunks of cardboard and tape them into a triangle around your body. Cover in yellow or orange duct tape.

30-second costume:
Groucho

Black duct tape gives you the look of big greasepaint eyebrows and mustache. Got some extra time? Make yourself an odor-free cigar using brown duct tape.

"Hey, Tim. I made one of those duct tape cigars and it was anything but odor-free!"

"You're not supposed to light it, Jim!"

"Oh."

Human Bird Feeder

Leave some treats for the trick-or-treating birds by placing birdseed on strips of duct tape and hanging them from tree branches.

Make yourself a sticky-side-out duct tape vest and cover it in birdseed. Stand in your yard and wait for birds to land on you and start pecking. Once several are feeding, bring them trick-or-treating or to the Halloween party with you.

"Okay, I've got a good one this time, Tim. Duct tape paper lunch bags over your entire body."

"Why, Jim?"

"You can go to the party as a lunch lady. Or a bag lady. Yeah, that's better."

"No, it's not."

Referee

Dress in black and use white duct tape to create vertical stripes on your shirt (or white with black stripes). Don't forget to hang a whistle around your neck.

Jailbird

712353

Same as the referee costume, but make the stripes horizontal rather than vertical. Then make a duct tape ball and chain to shackle around your ankle.

A new twist on bobbing for apples: Wrap party guests' heads with sticky-side-out duct tape and send them headfirst into a bin filled with plastic balls. The contestant who comes out with the most balls stuck to their headband wins.

Bumble Bee

Cover a black turtleneck with horizontal yellow duct tape stripes. Complete the outfit with silver duct tape wings on the back and a black duct tape "stinger" pointing off your butt.

Computer Geek (or Nerd)

Party Idea

Wrap all of your snack-size candy bars in duct tape (over their original wrappers). Then, play a guessing game: Which type of candy bar hides under the duct tape wrapper? Winners not only get to eat their candy, but all of the previously mis-guessed bars as well.

Make a duct tape pocket protector and put duct tape on the bridge of your glasses. Not washing your hair for a few days prior to the event will add to the realism. To achieve the Bill Gates look, stuff wads of money in each of your pockets.

95

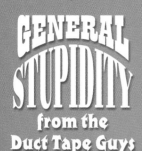

GENERAL STUPIDITY
from the
Duct Tape Guys

Can't decide on a costume? Duct tape a full-size mirror to the front of you and go as everyone else at the party.

Pink Flamingo

Cover yourself in pink duct tape and tape one foot to your butt. A yellow hooked beak built onto the bill of a pink-taped baseball cap finishes off the head.

Note: There is NO need to put a stick up your backside like those lawn ornaments have.

Moral Fiber

Duct tape a couple of gray "stone" Ten Commandment tablets and carry them around while wearing a box of bran flakes duct taped to your head. Or attach a long, white duct tape beard and you'll look like Moses.

Pumpkin Carvin'?
Want a jack-o'-lantern without the mess? Just apply black duct tape shapes to the sides of your chosen gourd. This is also a good way to test your design before you actually cut it into the pumpkin.

Game Show Contestant

Fashion a contestant podium from cardboard, cover with brightly colored duct tape, and put your name on the front. Secure this around your lower torso. Ring a buzzer or bell every time you would like to talk or answer a question.

30-second costume:
Pinocchio

Wrap beige duct tape to form a nose extension.

30-second costume:
Taxi Driver

Duct tape a beaded seat cushion to your back. Put on your best De Niro impersonation, "Are you talkin' to me?"

Note: To add to your outfit, make a name tag with your photo and a multi-syllabic, unpronounceable last name.

Roadkill

Tire Sniper

Get some bubble wrap with one-inch bubbles (at most office supply stores or in dumpsters behind gift shops—bigger bubbles work better). Cut a strip about 18 inches long and the width of a tire. Tape this to the tread of the tire of a parked car. When the car starts moving, the resultant popping sounds like a machine gun.

Use duct tape to create large tire-track designs running across your clothing. (Cartoon-style dead eyes and tongue optional.)

101

Frankenstein

Note: Duct taping blocks to the bottom of your shoes will add to your height and to your awkward Frankenstein walk.

Green and black duct tape and a bit of cardboard are all you need to create an authentic-looking Frankenstein headpiece. Add some silver duct tape for neck bolts.

Life of the Party

Cover a sticky-side-out duct tape vest with pieces of Life cereal. Wear the box as a hat. Presto! You are the "Life of the Party" (no lampshade required).

Sinking Chair

Here's a prank you can pull on your teacher or coworkers. Under pneumatic desk chairs there's usually a height adjustment lever. Tape this lever down so it releases the pressure. When pressure is placed on the seat, it will go down very quickly.

Duct Tape Man

Our favorite superhero costume! Use duct tape to fashion a mask and cape, then cover an old pair of tights or long johns with duct tape (don't skip the tights if you're attached to the hair on your legs). Make a big duct tape "D" on the front of your shirt. Break the ice with other party-goers by "tagging" them (sticking small swatches of duct tape to their persons).

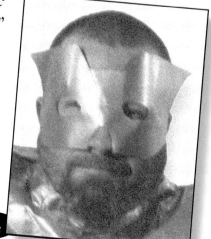

Junk Drawer

Once your junk drawer is cleaned out by making the Junk Drawer costume, ensure that it stays clean—just duct tape the drawer shut.

A duct tape vest, sticky side out, adorned with paper clips, coupons, empty tape dispensers, toothpicks, and used pens and pencils turns you into a human junk

105

Witch

A Halloween classic. Black duct tape over a paper cone makes a good witch's hat. Black duct tape over a dress and coat with tattered sleeves and hems adds to the look. Use the tape to blacken out a few teeth (dry your teeth off before applying). Don't forget your broom.

Road Worker

Make the witch's hat out of orange duct tape, accessorize it with a bright orange duct tape vest, and replace the broom with a shovel—you're a road worker!

Missing Link

Note: Actual arm extended another foot or so with duct tape and a rubber hand or glove.

Duct tape arm extenders onto the end of each arm, long enough so the knuckles drag on the ground when you walk. Combine this costume with the Wolfman (page 17) and you may look like one of those Big Foot/Sasquatch things.

Moo Boo

Dress entirely in white and cover yourself with large, black duct tape spots and you're a Holstein. Make the spots smaller and accessorize with a red duct tape collar and you're a Dalmatian.

SCARE TACTICS

Creepy Fingers

Hang duct tape strips, folded over onto themselves, sticky side in, from the ceiling of a hallway. Turn off the lights. When trick-or-treaters walk through the hallway, the duct tape "fingers" will brush against their hair.

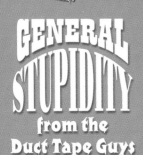

"Hey, that's more than 101 costumes, Tim!"

"We can't take any out now, Jim, the book's already been printed!"

"Let's throw in a few more and people will get way more than they paid for."

"Excellent idea, Jim."

Monk

Clothe yourself in a long, black duct tape-hooded robe, attach a little duct tape halo to your head, and you're a monk.

Human Vending Machine

Duct tape empty pop cans to yourself and go to your Halloween party as a human vending machine. Or use full pop or beer cans and pick up extra money by actually selling the beverages.

30-second costume:
Einstein

Duct tape a mop to your head and a big, white duct tape walrus mustache to your upper lip.

Let Your Imagination Run Wild!

Einstein said, "Imagination is more important than knowledge." We agree! No matter what idea your imagination can dream up, you can probably make it out of duct tape. At Halloween, or any time of year, duct tape is fashion design on a roll. Here, Amber and Jana proudly display their duct tape fashion show creations.

Invisible Wall

Duct tape plastic cling wrap across the doorway of a very dimly lit room and wait for some unsuspecting victim to enter.

Jim and Tim

Dress up in duct tape–enhanced clothing and wear dark glasses or goggles. Go trick-or-treating as Jim and Tim, the Duct Tape Guys.

"That's what I'm going trick-or-treating as this year, Tim."

"Me too, Jim."

Heavy-Duty Trick-or-Treat Bag

Whoops! We almost forgot the most important tool used to trick-or-treat: the trick-or-   treat bag! Make a heavy-duty bag by duct taping over a paper grocery sack in a color of duct tape that matches your costume. A long strap can be slung over your shoulder to help you carry your load.

Note: Duct tape flashlights and reflectors onto your bag for extra visibility.

Production Shots

Trimming the "Invisible Man"

Scott, our photographer and videographer.

Jim, typecast as cheese.

Grabbing video of the Halloween shoot. (Look for it on our web site.)

Supply Information

Lots of people ask us where you can get colored duct tape. Duck® brand duct tape has a nice assortment of colors (they provided all of the tape you see in this book). Check out our web site for an up-to-date listing of retail outlets for colored duct tape. Click to: www.ducttapeguys.com/retail

Duct Tape Online

If you like duct tape and you haven't discovered our web site, set aside a week or so, because this site is MASSIVE! We've been gathering duct tape uses since 1994. Fashions, art, medical, camping, auto repair, home improvement, and some uses too bizarre to categorize . . . they are all there!

Aunt Dinah's Duct Tape Diner is the place to share your unique duct tape uses with the world. You also can see a video about the birth of duct tape, watch clips from our television show appearances, flip through our duct tape cartoon collection, hear Jim and Tim's early-day radio shows, "Duct Tape Talk," learn creative thinking techniques, sign up for our e-newsletter, get your hands on free stuff, and enter our contests . . . .

All this and a ton more at:
ducttapeguys.com. Stop by soon!

Books, Videos, T-Shirts...

If you liked this book, you'll probably love our other "breathtakingly stupid" creations as well! In bookstores now, you can find *The Jumbo Duct Tape Book* and *Duct Shui*, as well as our video, *Duct Tape: The Video*.

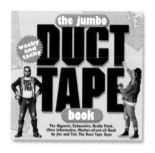  

Searching for our books or video and don't live near a bookstore? *The Original Duct Tape Pro Shop* allows you to get our stuff online!

Not only can you get our books and videos, but we have an absolutely HUGE variety of T-shirt designs for duct tape and humor enthusiasts of all ages.

Visit the Pro Shop today at:
ducttapeguys.com/store

About the Authors

The Duct Tape Guys are brothers-in-law Jim Berg (Elvis) and Tim Nyberg (Groucho). Neither had a clue that a 1994 power outage at a family Christmas Eve gathering would lead to a career based on duct tape. Jim, then a kindergarten teacher, told the gathering that if he knew where the power outage was, he could probably fix it with duct tape. Being brought up on "lesser tapes," Tim, a graphic designer and illustrator, asked Jim what he meant by "Fix it with duct tape?" Jim's wife explained that Jim fixed pretty much everything with duct tape and started listing off uses for the tape. Tim thought, "There's a book in here!" He grabbed his laptop (battery fully charged) and the whole family sat around in the candlelight brainstorming uses for duct tape.

This is the authors' sixth book since their original 1994 book, *The Duct Tape Book*. The guys also write the *365 Days of Duct Tape* Page-A-Day® Calendars, have produced a video, and are featured on hundreds of radio and television shows each year. They appear throughout North America and Europe doing their bizarre duct tape stand-up comedy at home and garden shows, colleges, comedy clubs, and corporate events.